The CROSSING

HOW GEORGE WASHINGTON SAVED THE AMERICAN REVOLUTION

JIM MURPHY

SCHOLASTIC PRESS ◆ NEW YORK

ISBN 978-0-439-69187-1

10 9 8 7 6 5 4 3 2 1   16 17 18 19 20

Printed in the U.S.A.   81
First printing 2016

The display type was set in Adobe JensonPro Semibold.
The text was set in Berkeley Oldstyle Book.
Maps on pages 21, 28, 43, 47, 61, 70, and 73 by Jim McMahon
Book design by Marijka Kostiw

SPECIAL THANKS TO STEVEN DIAMOND, NICOLE DURRANT, AND DIANE ALLFORD
FROM SCHOLASTIC'S PHOTO RESEARCH DEPARTMENT, AND TO BROWN UNIVERSITY
LIBRARY CENTER FOR DIGITAL SCHOLARSHIP FOR THEIR TENACIOUS WORK
IN TRACKING DOWN THE ART. AND TO KYLE F. ZELNER, ASSOCIATE PROFESSOR,
DEPARTMENT OF HISTORY, UNIVERSITY OF SOUTHERN MISSISSIPPI, FOR HIS
METICULOUS FACT CHECKING AND CONSULTATION OF THE MANUSCRIPT AND ART.

Visit the author at www.jimmurphybooks.com

To Beth and Mark Holechek—

great friends, wonderful neighbors,

and two of the most energetic,

generous, and creative people

I've ever met

—J. M.

CONTENTS

ON APRIL 19, 1775, British and American soldiers

clashed in a bloody battle in Massachusetts. Part of it happened in the village of Lexington, while the other part took place fifteen miles away in Concord. These first shots that started the American Revolution were the result of many years of anger, frustration, and growing hostility over how Great Britain governed   and taxed its American colonies.

As news of the fighting spread, thousands of armed and   determined Americans rushed to the area to aid their fellow colonists. Soon,   800 British soldiers found themselves under heavy fire and in full retreat. Even when reinforced by over 900 soldiers, the British had to fight their way back into Boston. In the end, more than 250 British soldiers were killed or wounded. By morning, Boston was surrounded by American forces, with the British soldiers trapped inside.

After the Battles of Lexington and Concord, American militiamen follow and shoot at retreating British troops attempting to make it to the safety of Boston.

TO ALL BRAVE, HEALTHY, ABLE BODIE
DISPOSED YOUNG MEN,
IN THIS NEIGHBOURHOOD, WHO HAVE ANY INCLINATION
NOW RAISING UNDER
GENERAL WASHINGTON,
FOR THE DEFENCE OF THE
LIBERTIES AND INDEPENDEN
OF THE UNITED STATES,
Againſt the hoſtile deſigns of foreign enemies,

TAKE NOTI

THAT *tueſday, wedneſday thurſday friday and*
Middleſex Lieutenant Reading with his muſic and recruiting party of
Battalion of the 11th regiment of infantry, commanded by Lieutenant Colonel Aaron Ogden, to
ſuch youth of SPIRIT, as may be willing to enter into this HONOURABLE ſervice.

The ENCOURAGEMENT at this time, to enliſt, is truly liberal and generous, namely, a bounty of T
ſupply of good and handſome cloathing, a daily allowance of a large and ample ration of proviſions,
and SILVER money on account of pay, the whole of which the ſoldier may lay up for himſelf and frienc
comfort are provided by law, without any expence to him.

Thoſe who may favour this recruiting party with their attendance as above, will have an opportuni
manner, the great advantages which theſe brave men will have, who ſhall embrace this opportunity of
different parts of this beautiful continent, in the honourable and truly reſpectable character of a ſoldier,
home to his friends, with his pockets FULL of money and his head COVERED with laurels.

Once the war had begun, the representatives of the thirteen original colonies at the Continental Congress were faced with a major decision. Who would organize the ragtag group of rebellious men into a real army and lead it in the fight against Great Britain? To answer that question, these representatives assembled in Philadelphia in June.

Everyone understood that the decision of who would command the American army was vitally important. The British forces had been whipped badly on April 19 and forced to retreat, but they hadn't surrendered. They would fight back, and they would seek revenge. The representatives in Philadelphia knew that the American commander would not only be responsible for the fate of the army and the lives of its soldiers, he would hold the entire future of the country in his hands.

A 1775 recruiting poster that promised many things, including a twelve-dollar bounty and the opportunity "of spending a few happy years in viewing the different parts of this beautiful continent."

THE COMMANDER

GEORGE Washington rode into Philadelphia on a warm June morning, the hooves of his chestnut-colored horse clip-clopping on the cobblestone street. He dismounted near the State House and gave the reins of his horse to William Lee, his slave and close companion, who accompanied Washington everywhere during the war.

Washington stood six feet two inches tall and looked dashing in the blue-and-buff-colored uniform of the Virginia militia company that he led. As he walked toward the State House, he had a no-nonsense look to him. He appeared, wrote a delegate's wife who saw him, "as awful as a god."

He was an important person in general, but on June 15, he was thinking about a serious issue being discussed by Congress. The day before, one of the Massachusetts representatives, John Adams, had suggested that Washington be chosen to command the Continental army.

Other men had been mentioned for the job, but it was Washington who intrigued most of the representatives. As one from Connecticut pointed out, Washington was "no harum-scarum, ranting, swearing

George Washington looking quite dashing in his uniform. To the right is William Lee, his slave and constant companion during the war. (THE METROPOLITAN MUSEUM OF ART)

fellow, but sober, steady, and calm." He also had a good deal of military experience.

During the French and Indian War (1754–1763), Washington had commanded several hundred Virginia men for more than three years. He had led his men well, but his record was hardly perfect. He was with General Edward Braddock and his 1,700 soldiers in western Pennsylvania when they were ambushed and routed by a smaller number of French soldiers

and Native Americans. And he was in command when he suffered a humiliating defeat at Fort Necessity in the Ohio territory.

There were other problems as well. Washington had never commanded more than 5,000 men at a time, did not know how to position artillery or maneuver cavalry, and had no engineering skills in building defensive positions. When compared to the British officers he would face, he was, in the words of one historian, "a rank amateur."

After much consideration, the delegates to Congress followed John Adams's advice to overlook these flaws, adding that Washington's appointment "will have a great Effect in cementing and securing the Union of these Colonies." Congress then voted unanimously to make him commander of the newly formed Continental army.

The only person uncertain about his appointment was George Washington himself. After the vote was taken, he turned to fellow Virginian patriot Patrick Henry and said, "Remember,

When Washington took command of the troops near Boston, he found them to be undisciplined, rude, and certainly not dressed in uniforms as portrayed in this romanticized 19th-century painting. (ANNE S. K. BROWN MILITARY COLLECTION, BROWN UNIVERSITY LIBRARY)

Mr. Henry . . . from the day I enter upon the command of the American armies, I date my fall, and the ruin of my reputation."

Washington rode out of Philadelphia to join his men in Boston several days later, already planning his military strategy. When the British left Boston — and he had no doubt that would happen by spring 1776 — he would move his men and all their equipment to New York, where he felt sure the British would attack next. Whoever occupied New York, Washington knew, could control the roads between the northern and southern colonies over which supplies and soldiers would travel.

Relocating his army would be the easy part. His other tasks would be nearly impossible to accomplish: He had to shape untrained farmers and shopkeepers into skilled soldiers and then defeat the greatest military power in the world. The entire fate of a young country rested squarely on his shoulders.

The weight of his responsibility was still troubling him when he wrote to his wife, Martha, about becoming the commander of the American forces. "You may believe me my dear Patsy, when I assure you . . . I have used every endeavor in my power to avoid it . . . from a consciousness of its being a trust too great for my capacity." In the weeks and months ahead, his capacity to lead the revolution would be tested again and again.

THE INVASION

GEORGE Washington was awakened at his headquarters in lower Manhattan in New York City very early on the morning of August 22, 1776. The British were up to something, his staff officers told their commander. Hundreds and hundreds of soldiers were being loaded onto landing barges.

A drawing of a portion of the British fleet at anchor between Long Island (foreground) and Staten Island (to the left in the background), with another warship approaching in the distance. (THE NEW YORK PUBLIC LIBRARY, ASTOR, LENOX AND TILDEN FOUNDATIONS)

Washington made his way to the top of a building where he could just barely see the masts of the British ships in the distance. Almost three months had passed since the British had first sailed into the waters between Staten Island and Long Island. It was an awesome display of military power that consisted of 73 warships, 344 transport vessels, 32,000 soldiers, 15,000 seamen, and more than 1,200 pieces of artillery. One astonished rooftop observer remembered "the whole Bay was full of shipping. . . . I thought all of London was afloat." Now, at last, the British were about to launch the largest invasion in their history.

For more than a year, Washington had nervously awaited and prepared for this day. In that time, he'd managed to move his 19,000 soldiers from Massachusetts to New York and to erect a series of solid stone and timber barricades and small forts in and around the city.

The problem was, Washington had no idea where the British would strike. This forced him to do something that went against his most basic military training: He divided up his army. With the British about to launch a massive attack, Washington's men were scattered all around Manhattan Island, Long Island, and along the New Jersey side of the Hudson River.

At nine o'clock in the morning, a cannon boomed from the deck of a British warship. Immediately, thousands of oars dipped into the bay's calm waters as the flotilla of 500 British barges was set in motion. In a matter of minutes, it became clear that they were headed for Long Island.

Hundreds of British barges packed with soldiers, artillery, and supplies head for Long Island on August 22, 1776. (BROOKLYN HISTORICAL SOCIETY)

The first troops ashore were fast-moving light infantry and cavalry. Because the Americans hadn't anticipated the location of the landing, only 300 Continental soldiers from Pennsylvania were there to challenge the invaders. A quick charge by the British cavalry easily drove off the Americans, and the landing then proceeded without interruption.

The main body of troops came ashore next, followed by hired soldiers from Germany, known as Hessians. As each barge was unloaded, the men formed into neat lines and marched into the wooded countryside. In the hours ahead, 22,000 soldiers, plus artillery, supplies of food, ammunition, wagons, and horses were put ashore, ready to conquer America.

At that time, the American Revolution was still in its infancy. It had been just seventeen months since the fatal clashes at Lexington and Concord launched the war. The Declaration of Independence — the document in which Congress boldly declared the colonies to be free and independent from Great Britain — had been adopted only fifty days before. George Washington understood that "the hour is fast approaching on which the Honor and Success of this army and the safety of our bleeding Country depend."

Washington's biggest concern was that he didn't think his army could survive the coming British attack. It wasn't simply that his men were outnumbered and scattered all around New York. It was the men themselves.

After the Battle of Lexington and Concord, the American forces had driven the British back into Boston. They then used the hills surrounding Boston to lay siege to the city and the British army. The Battle of Bunker Hill, the biggest fight of the siege, saw 1,150 British soldiers killed or wounded. Eventually, what was left of the haggard British army, plus more than 1,000 Loyalist supporters of Great Britain, admitted they could not dislodge the Americans and fled Boston for the safety of Canada.

It seemed to Congress and the soldiers themselves that the Continental army was invincible. It had, after all, taken on the most powerful army in the world and sent it packing in humiliation. John Adams was so confident of victory that he gave a toast claiming it would be "a short and violent war." George Washington knew better.

His men had fought valiantly up in Boston, but they were still largely untrained amateurs who lacked battle experience. They were also, for the most part, undisciplined and unruly. Brawls, drunkenness, and insubordination were so common that one officer grumbled, "there never was a more mutinous and undisciplined set of villains." The men took particular delight in firing off their guns in town at all hours of the day and night.

Worse, as far as Washington was concerned, was that "the principles of democracy so universally prevailed" among his men that they often refused to follow orders. "Men accustomed to unbounded freedom, and no control," Washington lamented, "cannot brook the restraint which is indispensably necessary to the good Order and Government of an Army."

On top of this, the officers Washington relied on to carry out his orders were in a state of disarray. Most of them, Washington observed, "are the most indifferent kind of people I ever saw." Even his more reliable

THE DEATH OF WARREN

This print from 1775 depicts how American forces at Bunker Hill wore their everyday clothing instead of uniforms.

officers often disappointed him. The man who had planned the defense of Brooklyn, for instance, was too ill to command the troops there. The general who replaced him was so inexperienced that he did not know the Long Island terrain and wasn't sure what sort of plan had been put into effect.

The American army faced a formidable, well-trained, and battle-hardened army commanded by experienced officers. At the head of the British force was General William Howe. Washington knew him as a fierce and courageous fighter, an inspiring leader, and one of the best field generals in the British army. Washington had the gloomy sense that the fight in New York was going to be much harder than the one in Boston.

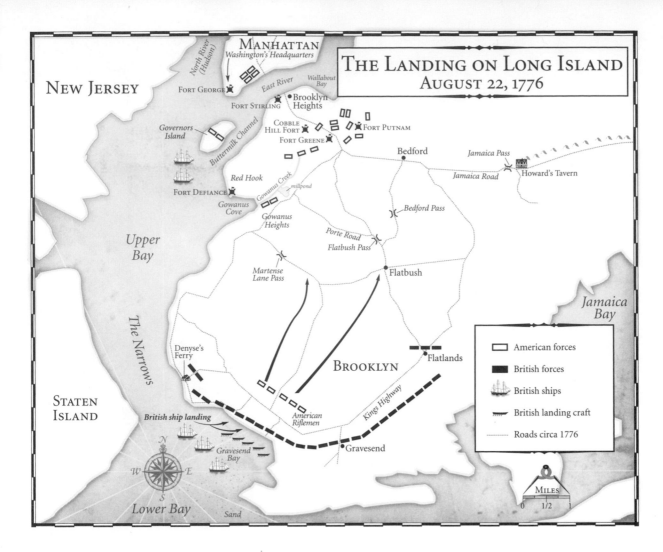

THE LANDING ON LONG ISLAND
AUGUST 22, 1776

This map shows the landing spot and position of British and American troops after the initial landing on August 22, 1776. As the village of Brooklyn grew larger during the 19th century, historians began referring to this as the Battle of Brooklyn.

By nightfall of August 22, the British army had campfires burning in an eight-mile arc that stretched from Denyse's Ferry to Jamaica Bay. Everything, a pleased General Howe noted, was going exactly according to plan.

Over on the American side, Washington spent a restless night discussing the coming fight with his senior officers. Unfortunately, his scouts and local spies were not sending him much reliable information about the

21

enemy troops in Long Island. Washington didn't know how many British soldiers had been landed or whether this was the main attack force. It was possible that Howe hoped to trick Washington into sending most of the American troops to Long Island, but that he really intended to land his main force in Manhattan.

The only thing George Washington knew for certain was that King George III and Parliament had issued strict orders to General Howe: Annihilate the Continental army and crush the spirit of revolution in the colonies. All Washington could do was sit tight and wait for the next British move.

George Washington and his senior officers study a map of New York City and Long Island and discuss their military options. (THREE LIONS/GETTY IMAGES)

CHAPTER 3
THE ATTACK

GEORGE Washington expected the British to attack immediately, but they didn't. In the days following the landing, Howe spent his time slowly working out the details of the attack and cautiously moving men into position. The delay made Washington nervous.

To be honest, Washington still had no idea what the British might be planning. The reason for Washington's confusion was simple: The area's rolling hills and tangled forests made it hard for his scouts to accurately count British troops there. Instead of reporting that 22,000 enemy soldiers had been landed, Washington was told that about 9,000 were on Long Island.

Washington then made the situation even worse. He decided not to send 400 cavalry troops to Long Island to scout out

enemy positions. His reason, he explained later, was because he thought it would be too costly to feed the horses. To gather information about the enemy he ordered the local militia cavalry to patrol the area. Unfortunately, the leader of the militia group had ridden off with his men without telling Washington.

A panoramic view of Brooklyn Heights (in the foreground) with American soldiers assembled in the near center. Buildings in lower Manhattan can be seen beyond the hilltop at the right. (THE NEW YORK PUBLIC LIBRARY)

A nervous Washington visited Brooklyn several times to check out the defenses and was appalled by what he found. Soldiers were wandering off on their own to take potshots at the British troops. "We shall have our men so scattered," an annoyed Washington wrote in a report, "& (more than probable) without ammunition, that the consequences must prove fatal to us."

The general in charge of the defensive positions on Brooklyn Heights was embarrassed enough to admit that "troops were wandering about western Long Island, sometimes miles beyond their position."

To end the chaos, Washington replaced this commander with the pugnacious general Israel Putnam. Putnam moved nearly 4,000 American soldiers forward to guard the main passes that led to the fortifications on Brooklyn Heights. Putnam also did his best to maintain discipline, but he was frustrated by another decision made by Washington. Most of Putnam's senior officers had been ordered to stay in New York City to sit in a court-martial of an officer who had been caught selling information to the enemy.

Despite the confusion in the field, Washington went back to his headquarters on August 26, convinced that his 10,000 troops could hold off a British attack. Sadly, his optimism was based on the incorrect estimate of enemy troop strength.

Major General Israel Putnam tried to organize the defenses on Long Island but found the task daunting.

(ANNE S. K. BROWN MILITARY COLLECTION, BROWN UNIVERSITY LIBRARY)

Washington had barely gone to sleep that night when the sound of musket fire was heard in the distance. At first, the officers at headquarters thought it was just a few soldiers idly shooting at one another. When the volume of musket fire suddenly increased and several cannons boomed, they realized something big was happening.

The sun was just beginning to rise as Washington and his staff leaped aboard boats to get to Brooklyn Heights. As they were being rowed across the East River, the British launched a massive three-pronged attack.

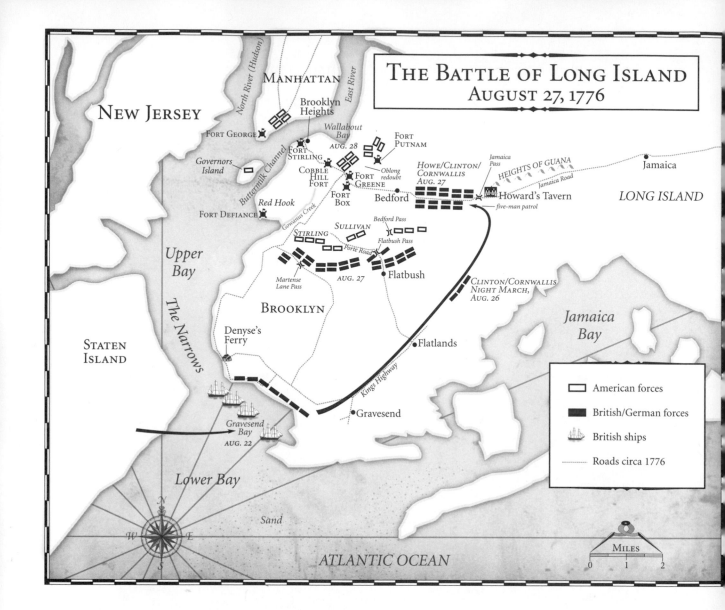

This map shows the four passes (Martense Lane Pass, Flatbush Pass, Bedford Pass, and Jamaica Pass) used by Howe's army to divide and surprise American forces.

The first assault came from the right side of the American line at Martense Lane. Five thousand British soldiers surged forward, driving back the small American force. Alerted by the increased musket volleys, 2,000 additional American soldiers rushed to meet the British.

Because these Americans held the high ground, they were able to drive off three British charges. At this point, the 4,000 Hessian troops at the Flatbush Pass began marching forward, their long bayonets glinting in the morning sun.

American colonel Samuel Miles had 500 men nearby and began hurrying them toward the fight. "I arrived within sight of the Jamaica Road," Miles recalled, "and to my mortification I saw the main body of the enemy in full march between me and our lines [at Brooklyn Heights]."

Quite simply, British general Howe had outfoxed George Washington. During the night, Howe had moved more than 10,000 troops north through the unguarded Jamaica Pass and positioned them on the Jamaica Road without being detected by the Americans. He had effectively divided Washington's army in two.

Miles saw that he and his men were outnumbered, so he attempted to flee through the woods. The British were waiting for him. Miles and half his men were captured, while the rest ran for the safety of the fortifications on Brooklyn Heights.

The remaining Americans at the Flatbush Pass suddenly saw that they were caught in a trap. Hessian artillery in front of their position was shelling them with deadly precision. Behind them, part of Howe's army was swarming toward them. The Americans broke and ran through the woods, hoping to get to Brooklyn Heights.

Next, the American soldiers near Martense Lane who had so stubbornly resisted the three British assaults were suddenly attacked from the rear by another group of Howe's soldiers. The Americans broke ranks and ran through a nearby marsh, then splashed across Gowanus Creek.

It was a sweet victory for the British, with more than 1,100 American soldiers either killed or wounded. One unidentified British officer proudly recalled, "it was a fine sight to see with what alacrity [we] dispatched the rebels with [our] bayonets, after we had surrounded them so they could not resist."

By this time, George Washington and his senior officers had made it to Brooklyn Heights. But instead of finding a stout American resistance, Washington was shocked to see hundreds and hundreds of his men running in panic. He rode forward to calm the troops pouring from the woods but found himself overwhelmed by mobs of breathless men.

In their panic, American soldiers retreat across Gowanus Creek. Many were shot attempting to swim to safety, while others drowned. (AUTHOR'S COLLECTION)

There was a wild scramble to get inside the protection of the fortifications, and many men were cut down from behind. Chaplain Philip Fithian was inside one of the forts and was devastated by what he saw. "O doleful! Doleful! Doleful!" he scribbled in his Bible. "Blood! Carnage! Fire! . . . Many, many we fear are Lost. . . . Such a dreadful Din my ears never before heard! — And the distressed wounded came crying into our lines."

Washington rode back to the American fortifications, angry and embarrassed by the way he had been outmaneuvered and by the way his men had acted. While some of his officers and soldiers had fought well, most had simply panicked and abandoned every forward American position. "The honor of making a brave defense," he noted sadly, "does not seem to be sufficient stimulus, when the success is very doubtful, and the falling into the enemy's hands probable."

As the sun went down on August 27, Washington rode along the American lines on Brooklyn Heights, trying to encourage his tired and beaten troops. When he looked out at the British lines, his heart must have sunk. The enemy was hard at work digging trenches to get closer to the fortifications. Washington was certain that Howe would try to deliver the killing blow in the morning.

Washington and his staff observing the Battle of Long Island

CHAPTER 4
THE ESCAPE

THE next morning, Washington and his men braced for the attack. But once again, General Howe did not send his troops forward. He continued digging trenches so his artillery would be very close to the American lines when a charge was finally ordered.

He may have delayed for three reasons. First, he had been at the Battle of Bunker Hill and knew firsthand how deadly the Americans could be with their muskets. Second, he was probably hoping that Washington would see the American army could never win an all-out battle, and that he would surrender. To some degree this idea was working. Hundreds of American soldiers had already deserted Washington and fled the area.

The third reason might have been the most important. General Howe wanted British warships to move into the East River behind the American troops. Once the ships were there, Washington and his men would be pinned between two powerful British forces.

The only thing that stopped Howe from trapping Washington's army was a fortunate wind. Just when the warships were about to sail, the wind changed direction and stalled them in the bay. Then, late in the day, dark clouds rolled in and a heavy rain began to fall.

Washington inspected his troops that night with a growing sense of

General William Howe, one of Britain's best field generals,
commanded the British forces in America during the Battle of Long Island.

doom. He knew that eventually the rain would stop, the wind would change direction again, and the British warships would sail into position. And it was clear that his men had very little fight left in them. As one tired soldier noted, they were "subject to almost incessant rains, without baggage or tents and almost without victuals or drink, and in some part of the lines the men were standing up to their middles in water."

George Washington was not the sort of general who ran from a fight. His military training and sense of honor told him that he should stand and face the enemy. Anything else would be cowardly. But his eyes told him that any fight would result in the massacre of his army. Washington then came to an important decision: He would retreat.

Washington made another decision as well. He would keep his plan a secret from all but his senior staff. The commander was worried that announcing an official retreat would cause his scared and bedraggled army to panic.

That evening, after dark, several companies were told to prepare for an assault on the British. One sixteen-year-old soldier named Joseph Plumb Martin was digging up turnips when the order came to march. "When I arrived," he recalled, "the men were all paraded to march off the ground; [I] seized my musket and fell into the ranks."

They then headed toward the ferry. "We were strictly enjoined not to speak, or even cough," Martin continued. "All orders were . . . communicated to the men in whispers. What such secrecy could mean we could not divine."

When they got to the ferry landing, it was very dark. No lamps were burning, and no one would tell them where they were going.

The men were loaded onto waiting boats and told to be quiet. The boats were being manned by skilled fishermen from Gloucester, Massachusetts, under the direction of Colonel John Glover. When everyone was in place, the boats rowed off as quietly as possible across the dark water toward Manhattan Island.

Colonel John Glover was in charge of the mariners who
rescued the American army trapped on Brooklyn Heights.

(HULTON ARCHIVE/GETTY IMAGES)

The evacuation went smoothly for an hour or so, but then the wind picked up and the water became dangerously choppy. Some boats were even pushed toward the British fleet. Fortunately, the wind calmed down before the boats were spotted, and the retreat proceeded.

Washington spent the evening riding between the ferry landing and

A dramatic portrait of Washington directing troops during the nighttime retreat from Brooklyn Heights (LIBRARY OF CONGRESS)

the fortifications on Brooklyn Heights. To fool the British, he had the men withdraw from the forts in a very precise way. "As one regiment left their station," one of Washington's staff recalled, "the remaining troops were moved to the right and left, and filled up the vacancies."

By the morning of August 29, nearly all of the American army, plus its horses, cannons, and ammunition, was safely on Manhattan Island. But that left more than 1,000 men still on Brooklyn Heights. It would be only minutes before the British realized what was happening and sent swarms of troops to attack the remaining rebels. Just then, another piece of amazing luck came drifting Washington's way.

"At about this time," an officer would later write, "a very dense fog began to rise, and it seemed to settle in a peculiar manner over both encampments. . . . [So] very dense was the atmosphere that I could scarcely discern a man at six yards' distance."

Under cover of this thick blanket of fog, the last remaining troops of the Continental army made their escape. One officer recalled that "Gen. Washington [was] on the ferry stairs when I stepped into one of the last boats that received the troops."

Many of those who participated in the escape felt that God had intervened to save them with wind, rain, and fog. Others gave George Washington the credit for organizing and carrying out a very difficult retreat while under the enemy's guns. In the end, more than 8,000 of the 10,000 soldiers in Brooklyn survived to fight another day — which was exactly what George Washington intended to have happen.

THE RETREAT

WHEN George Washington arrived back in New York City, his plan was to stand and fight the British there. "I conceive it my duty," he wrote to the president of the Congress, John Hancock, "to make head against [the enemy]." His men, however, were in no shape to take on the British and Hessian soldiers. As Pastor Ewald Shewkirk observed, "It seemed a general damp had spread [among them]. . . . Many looked sickly, emaciated, cast down."

Dissent was also brewing among his officers and troops. Many felt the fighting on Long Island had been badly managed and wondered if Washington should be replaced as commander. One colonel wrote to his representative in Pennsylvania to complain that "upon the whole, less Generalship never was shown in any Army since the Art of War was understood."

A growing number of those in Congress shared this opinion. The names of two other American generals, Charles Lee and Horatio Gates, surfaced as possible replacements of Washington. One signer of the Declaration of Independence, Benjamin Rush, felt that the leadership of "a Gates [or] a Lee . . . would in a few weeks render [the army] an irresistible body of men."

In the end, Congress backed off, worried that a change in command when the army was in peril would only cause more confusion among the troops. For the time being, George Washington would remain the commander of the Continental army.

Luckily for Washington, General Howe once again took his time preparing for the next assault. Howe's reason this time was that he wanted to set up long-range artillery on Brooklyn Heights with a clear shot at the city just across the water.

At first, John Adams supported Washington, but after the Battle of Long Island, he often urged that another officer be made commander. (LIBRARY OF CONGRESS)

When Washington saw the artillery, he realized his army would be easily blasted to pieces, and he came to another decision. He then moved most of his men north to Harlem Heights, where the high ground would give him the same advantage he had had during the siege of Boston.

But Washington was no longer commanding an aggressive, determined army. "Our situation is truly distressing," he wrote to Congress. "Til of late I had no doubt in my mind of defending this place, nor should I have yet if the Men would do their duty, but this I despair of."

He was, in fact, in charge of a retreating army. In the weeks following the Battle of Long Island, his army would be attacked by the British several times. There were a number of instances when his officers and men performed very well. In the end, however, Washington was always forced to retreat, often in panic, in the face of the powerful British army. Joseph Plumb Martin captured the overall feeling of the men when he observed that "the demons of fear and disorder seemed to take full possession of all."

Washington and most of his men fled Harlem Heights and headed farther north to White Plains. In the battle there, his army once again panicked and ran. Washington could only sigh and ask, "Are these the men with which I am to defend America?"

Next, he moved his army up to the rocky terrain of North Castle Heights. By this time it was October, and the weather was turning sharply colder. Howe then called off the chase and withdrew his army to winter in New York City.

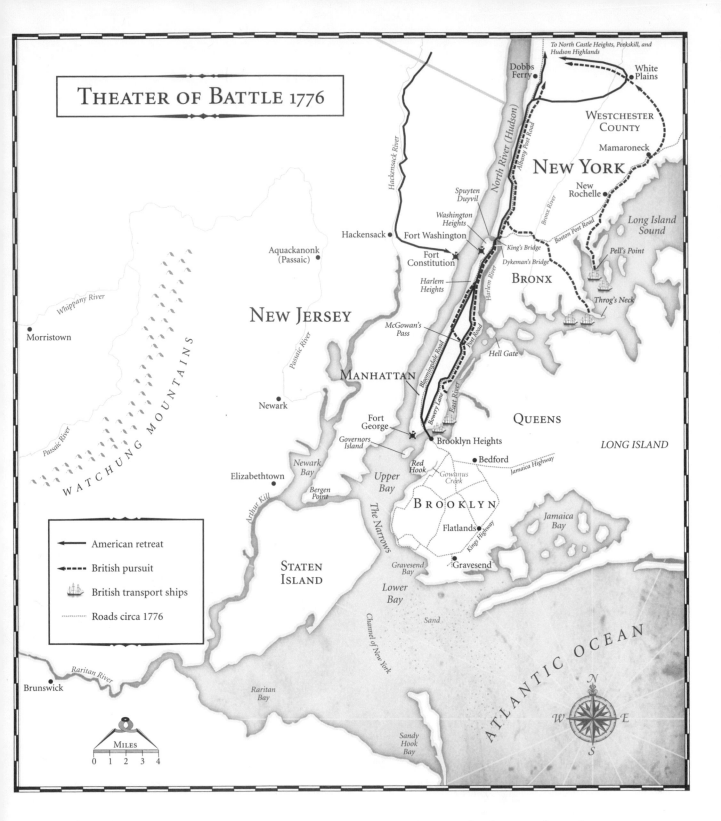

THEATER OF BATTLE 1776

To North Castle Heights, Peekskill, and
Hudson Highlands

Dobbs
Ferry

White
Plains

**WESTCHESTER
COUNTY**

Mamaroneck

NEW YORK

New
Rochelle

*Spuyten
Duyvil*

*Washington
Heights*

Fort Washington

King's Bridge

*Long Island
Sound*

Hackensack

Fort
Constitution

Dykeman's Bridge

Pell's Point

BRONX

*Harlem
Heights*

Harlem River

Throg's Neck

Aquackanonk
(Passaic)

Hackensack River

North River (Hudson)

Bronx River

Boston Post Road

Albany Post Road

Whippany River

NEW JERSEY

Passaic River

*McGowan's
Pass*

Post Road

Hell Gate

Morristown

MANHATTAN

Bloomingdale Road

East River

Bowery Lane

Newark

QUEENS

LONG ISLAND

Fort
George

Brooklyn Heights

*Governors
Island*

Bedford

Jamaica Highway

Elizabethtown

*Newark
Bay*

*Red
Hook*

*Gowanus
Creek*

*Bergen
Point*

*Upper
Bay*

B R O O K L Y N

*Jamaica
Bay*

Arthur Kill

Flatlands

Kings Highway

W A T C H U N G   M O U N T A I N S

LEGEND

→ American retreat

┅► British pursuit

⛵ British transport ships

⋯ Roads circa 1776

The Narrows

**STATEN
ISLAND**

*Gravesend
Bay*

Gravesend

*Lower
Bay*

Sand

Raritan River

Brunswick

*Raritan
Bay*

Channel of New York

A T L A N T I C   O C E A N

*Sandy
Hook
Bay*

MILES
0 1 2 3 4

N
W   E
S

This map shows the retreat of Washington's army up Manhattan Island, into White Plains,
and then back down to Fort Constitution (which is now known as Fort Lee).

Washington worried that Howe had other plans in mind. When Washington fled Manhattan Island, he had left a large number of men at Fort Washington and across the Hudson River in New Jersey at Fort Lee. He was certain that Howe would storm Fort Washington so that no American soldiers would be on the island during the winter. The 2,800 men there would stand no chance against the entire British army.

Sadly, Washington understood he was also fighting another powerful enemy now: desertion. In Boston, the men stayed to fight mainly because they outnumbered the British trapped in town. But now, the tables were turned. It was the Continental army that was being pursued by a large and relentless enemy. When Washington set off for New Jersey, one half of his army had already packed their bags and gone home.

"Great numbers of them have gone off," a disappointed Washington told Congress, "in some instances, almost by whole regiments, by half Ones & by Companies at a time."

Washington left 4,000 men in Peekskill, New York, and took approximately 3,000 down to Fort Lee, where another 2,000 soldiers were camped. Across the Hudson, the soldiers stationed at Fort Washington waited anxiously for the next move of the British.

Washington had barely gotten his tent up on November 16 when the British launched an all-out attack. After a two-hour artillery bombardment, approximately 13,000 British and Hessian soldiers swarmed toward Fort Washington from three directions.

A view of British and Hessian troops on the Harlem River as they land on northern Manhattan Island and begin their attack on Fort Washington.

(© THE NEW YORK PUBLIC LIBRARY/ART RESOURCE)

No accurate images exist of Margaret Corbin. But this painting of Molly Pitcher, a legendary heroine of the American Revolution, captures Corbin's determined and passionate spirit.
(© NIDAY PICTURE LIBRARY/ALAMY)

Five thousand Hessian soldiers landed at the north end of Manhattan Island and moved toward 500 American soldiers entrenched on a steep hill. This part of the battle lasted more than two hours, with the Hessians sustaining over 300 casualties. One of the fiercest American fighters on the hill was Margaret Corbin. After her husband was killed, Corbin took his place at his cannon and aimed with such deadly precision that her position came under heavy enemy fire. Only a severe shoulder wound forced Corbin from the battle.

Despite their strong defensive position, there simply weren't enough Americans to hold back the Hessian advance. A German officer would later proudly report that "every obstacle was swept aside, the earthen works broken through, the swamps waded, [the] rocks scaled and the riflemen were driven out of their breastworks." The American survivors of this attack retreated to the safety of Fort Washington.

To the south, several thousand British soldiers moved up the island, easily smashing through three American lines of defense. These Americans joined those in the north at Fort Washington.

Washington, accompanied by three senior officers, left Fort Lee and hurried across the Hudson at the first sound of the battle. At eleven o'clock, he was at the Robert Morris House, directing his troops, when the third wave of British soldiers landed nearby. A force of 800 came swarming up the hill just behind the Morris House.

A map showing the multipronged attack on Fort Washington.
George Washington was very nearly captured at the Morris House.

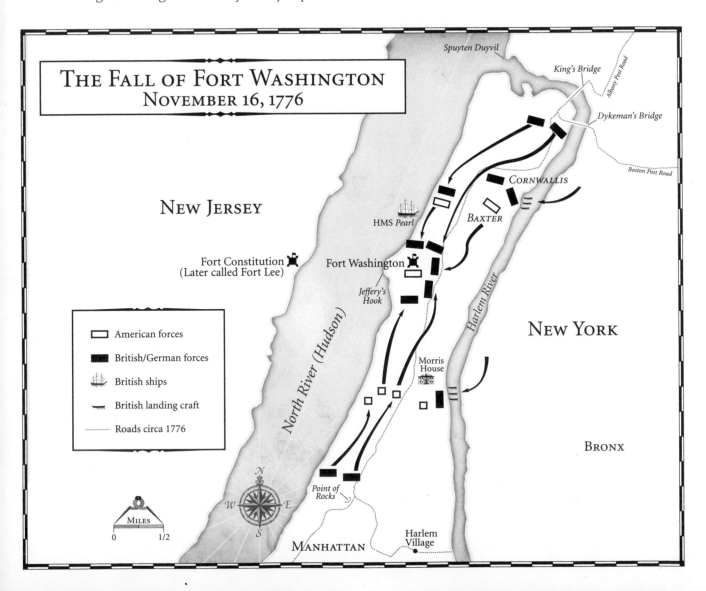

THE FALL OF FORT WASHINGTON
NOVEMBER 16, 1776

Spuyten Duyvil

King's Bridge

Albany Post Road

Dykeman's Bridge

Boston Post Road

CORNWALLIS

NEW JERSEY

HMS *Pearl*

BAXTER

Fort Constitution
(Later called Fort Lee)

Fort Washington

Jeffery's
Hook

Harlem River

NEW YORK

☐ American forces

■ British/German forces

⚓ British ships

〜 British landing craft

⋯ Roads circa 1776

North River (Hudson)

Morris
House

BRONX

MILES
0   1/2

N
W · E
S

Point of
Rocks

Harlem
Village

MANHATTAN

For a few awkward moments, Washington refused to flee to avoid capture because he thought it would seem cowardly. Fortunately for Washington, his senior officers persuaded him to leave just moments before the British captured the Morris House and the few Americans still defending it.

Washington made it back to Fort Lee, where he and his staff watched the final awful moments of the battle. More than 2,600 American soldiers, plus 230 of their officers, were now trapped inside Fort Washington. After a brief holdout, the officer in charge agreed to surrender.

"I feel mad, vexed, sick, and sorry," one senior American officer wrote to a friend. "This is the most terrible event; its consequences are justly to be dreaded."

Washington knew that he had not only lost a great number of brave soldiers, he might very well have lost the American cause. To preserve what he had left, he abandoned Fort Lee and took the remaining 5,000 men under his command west, toward Hackensack.

He might have hoped to rest his men, but General Howe then did something unusual for him. He wasted no time and immediately sent his army out to destroy what remained of the Continental army.

Washington hurried his men south just ahead of the advancing British forces. To lighten their load, his desperate soldiers abandoned cooking kettles, muskets, ammunition pouches, and unnecessary clothing as they staggered along. A New Jersey citizen recalled that these soldiers "looked ragged, some without a shoe to their feet, and most of them wrapped in their blankets."

British troops and artillery being landed by the steep, rocky cliffs on the New Jersey side of the Hudson on November 20, 1776, in pursuit of Washington and his troops. (EMMET COLLECTION, THE NEW YORK PUBLIC LIBRARY, ASTOR, LENOX AND TILDEN FOUNDATIONS)

Washington sent orders that the troops he'd left in the north join him in order to stop the British. Both General Lee and General Gates refused to move their men down to help. Lee made his feelings clear when he wrote to Gates that "a certain great man is most damnably deficient. . . . [U]nless something which I do not expect turns up we are lost." Both felt

Washington had blundered so badly that one of them should be appointed the new commander of the army.

As Washington's army retreated, men continued to desert him for the safety of their homes. By November 21, he had only 4,000 troops left under his command. When they finally crossed the Delaware River and entered Pennsylvania, a count revealed that another 1,000 American soldiers had deserted. One Philadelphia resident remembered seeing the haggard American soldiers stumbling along. It was, he told a friend, "the most hellish scene I ever beheld."

Howe halted his troops when he reached the Delaware River. He had no respect for Washington as a general or for the Continental army and assumed his army would continue to outfight the Americans once winter ended. He posted 1,400 Hessian soldiers at Trenton to keep an eye on the Americans and established sixteen other garrisons in New Jersey. Then he took the bulk of his army back to New York City.

Washington was safe from the British for the moment, but he knew other problems loomed before him. He understood that Congress was frustrated and worried by his military failures and that many representatives would try to have him replaced as commander of the Continental army. Even one of his most vocal supporters from the past, John Adams, now prayed, "Oh, Heaven! Grant Us one great Soul! One leading Mind [to] extricate the best Cause, from that Ruin which seems to await it."

General Charles Lee did not like being in Washington's shadow and spent a lot of time belittling him. (ANNE S. K. BROWN MILITARY COLLECTION, BROWN UNIVERSITY LIBRARY)

Maybe even more troubling was the fact that the enlistments of more than half of what was left of Washington's army would run out on New Year's Day. How many of these men would stay to fight? Washington must have wondered. Would there even be a Continental army at all come spring?

CHARLES LEE, Esq.
MAJOR GENERAL of the CONTINENTAL-ARMY in AMERICA.

THE CROSSING

EVEN after the British called off their campaign, things got worse for George Washington and the Revolution. Scores of once staunch patriots suddenly felt their lives and property threatened and backed away from the cause. Even a signer of the Declaration of Independence, Richard Stockton, gave "his word of honor that he would not meddle in . . . American affairs" and swore allegiance to King George III.

Congress began again to discuss the possibility of replacing Washington. General Lee was their favorite choice. But before a vote could be taken, another bit of luck came Washington's way. Lee foolishly wandered away from his troops and was captured by the enemy, thus saving Washington's job for the moment.

Friends in Congress told Washington how close he had come to being replaced and urged him to do something to win back their confidence. He also wanted to end the year in as positive a way as possible to encourage volunteers for his army. That meant a victory on the battlefield.

Richard Stockton was so worried after Washington's humiliating retreat through New Jersey that he denounced the American cause and pledged his allegiance to King George III.

(PRINCETON UNIVERSITY ART MUSEUM)

But with so many enlistments about to run out, what could he do? It was then he remembered the Hessian troops across the Delaware in Trenton.

Unlike in Long Island, where he had little reliable information about the enemy, Washington now made sure he had some very good spies prowling the countryside. They told him that the commander of the Hessian troops, Colonel Johann Rall, kept his men fully dressed at all times and on constant alert for an American attack. He also learned that Rall hadn't bothered to construct any fortifications around the town.

An engraving showing some of the Hessian soldiers who were garrisoned at Trenton

J. C. Müller fe.
(ex Donop 1767 – 84)
Knijphausen.

Washington decided to launch a surprise attack against the Hessian troops on the day after Christmas. And once again he decided to tell only a few senior officers about the plan, worried that the British might have their own spies nearby. That was why one American soldier, John Greenwood, was so confused when he was ordered to get ready to march at four o'clock in the afternoon on Christmas Day. "None but the first officer knew where we were going or what we were going about," he remembered, "for it was a secret expedition."

The weather had been cold all day. As Greenwood and the other soldiers moved toward the waiting boats, the sky darkened ominously, and an icy drizzle began to fall. When the boats finally pushed off, a cold, driving rain was coming down. Once again, John Glover's experienced seamen would row the crowded boats, though this time they had to contend with treacherous, ice-clogged water.

The plan called for Washington to lead 2,400 men across the Delaware, ten miles upriver from Trenton. Several thousand additional soldiers had finally arrived from the north, and these were divided into three groups with orders to cross downriver in hope of cutting off escape routes. Unfortunately, the wind and heavy ice in the river stopped these other groups from crossing. Washington didn't know it as he landed on the New Jersey shore, but he and his men would be all alone when they attacked the Hessians.

By four o'clock in the morning of December 26, all of the men had been safely landed, but Washington wasn't happy. The operation was four hours behind schedule. It would be light by the time they reached Trenton, so there would be little hope of surprising the Hessian garrison.

Wrapped in a long coat, Washington sat on a box and considered calling off the attack. To press on would be a risk, he realized, but retreating had its own dangers. "I was certain there was no making a Retreat without being discovered and harassed on [recrossing] the River," Washington later wrote. "I determined to push on at all events."

A dramatic but inaccurate painting of George Washington being rowed through the drifting ice. In addition to this being the wrong type of boat, Washington would have been seated during the crossing to avoid serious injury. This 1776 scene was painted by Henry Mosler around 1912.

(LIBRARY OF CONGRESS)

It was at this moment that another bit of troubling news came his way. After being ordered several more times to bring his men south, General Horatio Gates had finally arrived. But instead of joining Washington in the raid on Trenton, Gates left camp in a huff. He then met with members of Congress to condemn Washington's planned attack, saying it was much too risky. If his attack failed, Washington knew he would be relieved of command of the Continental army, and the Revolution might well collapse completely.

General Horatio Gates believed he would make a better commander than Washington.

As the men lined up, a small number of scouts were sent ahead. The main group followed slowly, hauling eighteen pieces of heavy artillery up steep hills and along dark, rutted dirt roads. To make traveling even harder, the rain suddenly changed to a heavy snowfall. One soldier complained, "we began an apparently circuitous march, not advancing faster than a child ten years old could walk, and stopping frequently, though for what purpose I know not."

At the tiny village of Birmingham, the long column was split into two. One went to the left along the Upper Ferry Road, while the other continued along the River Road. Washington went with the column on the upper road.

Washington and his aides directing the crossing of the Delaware River

The men were completely exhausted from the cold wind and blinding snow. Jackets and pants began to freeze. Washington rode back and forth along the column, encouraging his men to stay together and to "press on, press on, boys!"

As they approached one of the small outposts guarding the town, the sun had already come up. But the storm that had slowed his march now came to Washington's rescue. The bitter cold and snow had driven the exhausted Hessian guards indoors, where most of them were asleep.

A charge was immediately ordered, and three columns of American soldiers were soon rushing toward the small building. Washington led the troops in the center. When a groggy Hessian soldier stepped out of the building, an American fired at him. At the same time, Washington heard the deep-throated roar of artillery being fired on the other side of town. Against all odds, the Americans had caught the Hessians by complete surprise.

The Hessian soldiers acted quickly and professionally and began assembling in the center of town. Colonel Rall ordered his men to attack the heart of the American line on the hills to the north. He also ordered his artillery to open fire.

American artillery responded with a massive bombardment. Solid shot bounded along the main road, killing five horses and at least eight enemy gunners. This was followed by intense musket volleys. The

Hessians in the southern part of Trenton broke and fled across the Assunpink Creek.

While this was taking place, Rall had gotten several hundred soldiers through town to an apple orchard. Washington spotted this and ordered troops to occupy the hill above the orchard. Rall realized he was heading into a trap and wisely withdrew his men back into town.

A map showing the various places where American troops attempted to cross the ice-packed river. Washington's men made it across, but those below Trenton were never able to block the escape routes as planned.

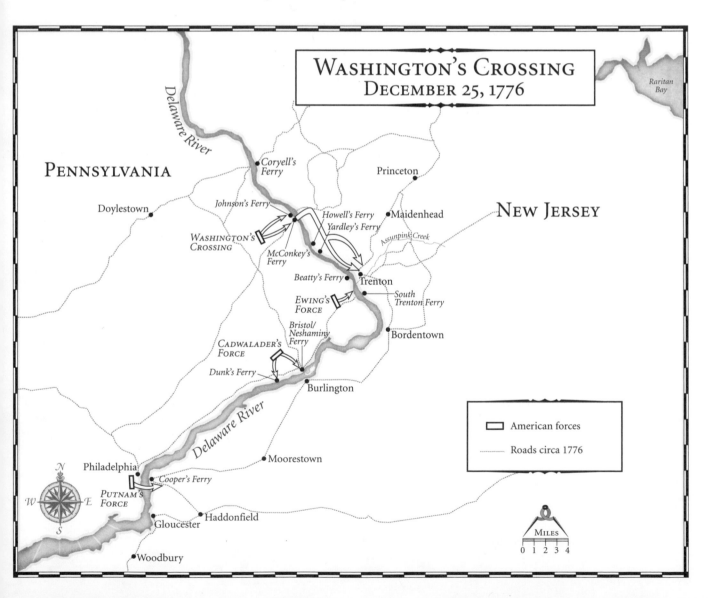

THE BATTL

American troops swarm into Trenton while the battle rages in the background.

OF TRENTON.

American soldiers had almost surrounded the town by this time, and many Hessian soldiers were killed or wounded. Four officers under Rall were hit, and when Rall stopped to encourage one of them, he was struck twice in the side and fell from his horse. The dying Hessian commander was carried to a nearby church.

The Hessian troops were in full retreat now, with American forces closing in fast. When they saw there was no way to escape, the Hessians lowered their company flags to the snow and tossed down their weapons.

American captain Thomas Forrest was about to unleash cannon fire into the enemy when he realized they were surrendering. "Sir," he said to George Washington, "they have struck."

"Struck!" Washington repeated, not fully understanding.

Washington accepts the surrender of Hessian troops at Trenton. The mortally wounded Colonel Johann Rall is in the center being held up by an American officer. The severely wounded officer just behind Rall is young Lieutenant James Monroe, who would become the fifth president of the United States. (YALE UNIVERSITY ART GALLERY)

"Yes, their colors are down."

Washington peered through the smoke and falling snow. "So they are," he finally said, urging his horse toward the Hessians.

While more than 400 of the enemy had eluded capture, The Battle of Trenton was as complete a victory as could be expected, considering the problems Washington and his men had encountered. When a senior officer rode up to report, Washington extended his hand. "Major," he said, smiling for the first time in months, "this is a glorious day for our country."

CHAPTER 7
THE OLD FOX

THE Battle of Trenton was a stunning victory for George Washington and the Continental army. Washington could have gone into winter quarters happy that he had preserved the Revolution at least until the spring. But Washington was too smart to think his work was done. He knew perfectly well that General Howe's sense of military honor wouldn't let him sit through the winter after such an embarrassing defeat.

As soon as he was back in Pennsylvania, Washington drew up a new plan: He wanted to recross the Delaware River, establish his forces on high ground that could be easily defended, and wait for the British to show up.

Almost immediately, a new problem confronted him. Even after he pleaded directly with his troops and offered a ten-dollar bonus to anyone who would stay, more than 2,600 of his men packed their bags and left camp. When his new expedition set out on December 29, Washington had only 3,300 men left under his command.

Washington was determined to make as strong a stand as possible and hope for the best. He took his men back to Trenton and crossed the

Assunpink Creek. The knoll there was very steep and had a clear view of the creek and the town. Only one narrow bridge led directly across the creek.

As the men began to put up log and stone barriers to protect themselves from enemy fire, spies brought Washington some unsettling information. Howe had dispatched a force of 8,000 British and Hessian troops under the command of one of his best officers, General Charles Cornwallis. What is more, they were already assembled at Princeton, only sixteen miles away.

Washington knew his troops would need many more hours to build good defensive barriers. So he sent 1,000 sharpshooters up the main road to Princeton to harass and slow the British advance.

In the past, his men had often panicked when faced with such overwhelming odds. But the men under his command were different now. The faint of heart had already abandoned the American cause, leaving behind men who were determined to stand and fight the enemy of their country. They had weathered many bad situations with George Washington and knew that he had suffered along with them. Besides, the Battle of Trenton had showed them what they could do if they stayed calm and followed orders.

His sharpshooters hurried up the main road and were able to meet the British force just outside of Princeton. They then fought a series of small but fierce battles that brought the British march to a complete halt five times. Even when the commanding officer of the American

General Charles Cornwallis was an experienced and intelligent commander who saw Washington and his tattered army as little more than a nuisance.

sharpshooters panicked and galloped away from the fighting, his men stood fast. By the time the British finally pushed into Trenton, it was five o'clock and the sun was setting.

George Washington and his troops were now fully dug in along the creek. Even so, many of the men were stunned to see the swarms of British and Hessian soldiers filling the landscape. As one officer later

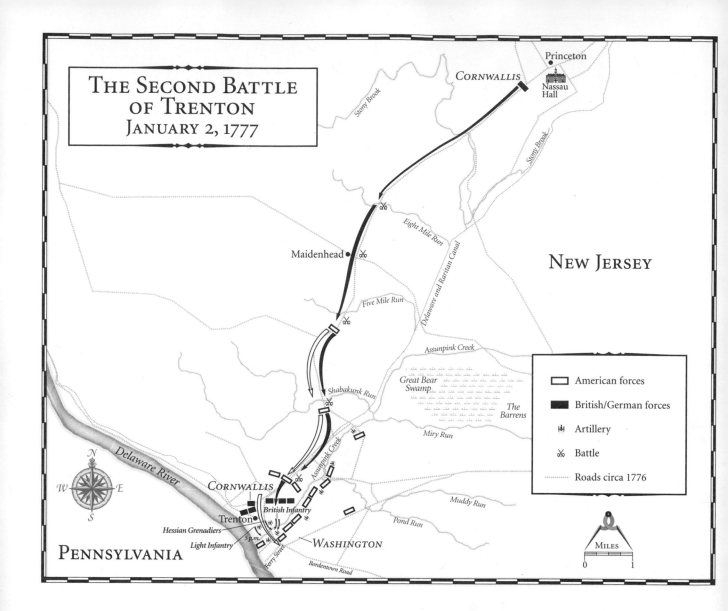

A map showing the British order of march from Princeton and the places where American sharpshooters delayed them. Washington's troops are lined up along the Assunpink Creek awaiting the British assault.

wrote, "If there ever was a crisis in the affairs of the Revolution, this was the moment."

Cornwallis decided to send four separate British columns across the creek. Three were going to attempt to cross at spots where the creek was shallow, while the fourth would try to storm the bridge.

The darkness made it difficult for the British to maneuver and see the Americans, who were now well concealed behind their log and stone barriers. Intense and accurate American shooting accompanied by savage artillery fire drove off every attempt to cross the water. The fighting was particularly brutal at the bridge.

A force of 300 British soldiers surged forward, hoping to seize the bridge. American sergeant Joseph White was at one of the nineteen cannons waiting to greet the enemy. "We let them come on some ways. Then . . . we all fired together. The enemy retreated off the bridge and formed again, and we were ready for them. Our whole artillery was again discharged at them."

The British regrouped and launched a third charge. "We let them come nearer," Sergeant White remembered. "We fired all [nineteen guns] together, and such destruction it made, you cannot conceive. The bridge looked red as blood, with their killed and wounded and red coats."

When his troops staggered away from the bridge, Cornwallis decided to call off further action for the night. Despite losing a great many men, the British commander was perfectly happy with the situation. "We've got the old fox now," he told his staff confidently about Washington. "We'll go over and bag him in the morning."

But the old fox wasn't about to be caught in the trap. Washington was pleased that his men had held off the British so decisively. But he was certain that in the morning Cornwallis would send waves and waves of soldiers against his men. The British might lose hundreds of them, but they would eventually wear down Washington's outnumbered troops and overwhelm them.

Washington could, of course, move his men south of Trenton down toward Burlington, where they could recross the Delaware to safety. This, Washington knew, would look too much like another retreat to Congress and the American people. This was something he wanted to avoid at all costs. That's when a senior officer mentioned a narrow back path that would take them around the British army and directly to Princeton.

Here was the solution Washington was looking for. He would take his little army and slip away from the large British force before him. He could then attack the few British soldiers who had been left behind at Princeton. This would avoid the impression that he was still commanding a retreating army.

At midnight, officers began telling their men to prepare to march. "Orders came by whispering," one sergeant recalled, "(not a loud word must be spoke) to form the line and march."

As quietly as possible, the men located the path and began moving through a tangled, dark wood. Some men became confused and lost in the dark; a group of 1,000 militiamen were so scared that they abandoned Washington and scampered south to Burlington.

In the past, losing so many men might have produced panic in those who remained. But the two victories at Trenton had showed them what could be accomplished if they stuck together. They stumbled along toward Princeton, barely able to stay awake but determined.

It took these men five hours to cover the eighteen miles to Princeton, and the sun was rising as they neared the unsuspecting British garrison.

This map shows the back route taken by Washington and his troops to Princeton and the spot where American and British troops first clashed.

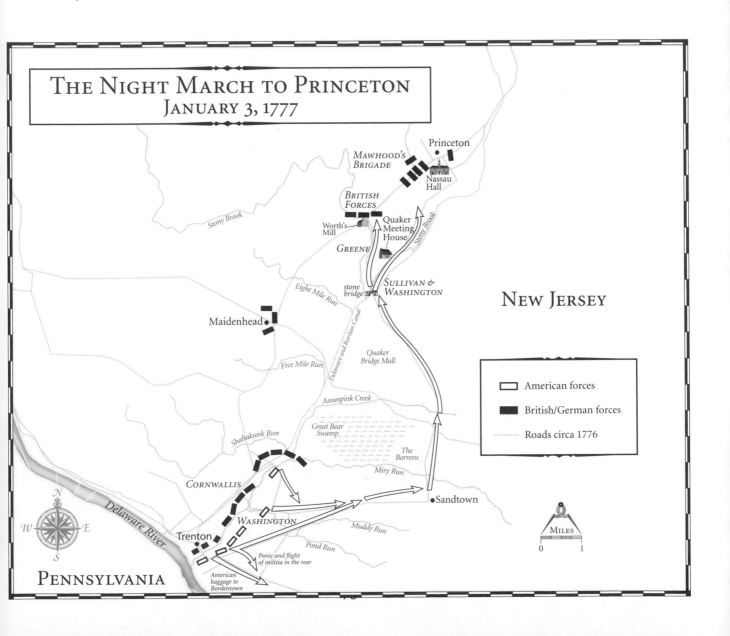

THE NIGHT MARCH TO PRINCETON
JANUARY 3, 1777

NEW JERSEY

Princeton

Mawhood's Brigade

Nassau Hall

British Forces

Worth's Mill

Stony Brook

Quaker Meeting House

Greene

Sullivan & Washington

stone bridge

Stony Brook

Maidenhead

Eight Mile Run

Delaware and Raritan Canal

Quaker Bridge Mall

Five Mile Run

Assunpink Creek

American forces

British/German forces

Roads circa 1776

Great Bear Swamp

The Barrens

Shabakunk Run

Miry Run

CORNWALLIS

Sandtown

Delaware River

WASHINGTON

Muddy Run

Trenton

Pond Run

Panic and flight of militia in the rear

American baggage to Bordentown

MILES

0   1

PENNSYLVANIA

Washington then split up his forces. He sent one under the command of General Hugh Mercer to attack the town from the main road, while he led the other up a back road to Princeton.

All seemed to be going according to plan when suddenly 800 British soldiers rushed from behind a hill and charged Mercer's soldiers. The battle that followed was brief but bloody, with each side firing several deadly volleys at the other. One American officer witnessed what was

The Battle of Princeton was brief but intense. This painting shows the chaos of hand-to-hand combat. (ANNE S. K. BROWN MILITARY COLLECTION, BROWN UNIVERSITY LIBRARY)

BATTLE OF PRINCETON—DEATH OF MERCER.

happening from a hill a half mile away. "My old associates were scattered about groaning, dying and dead," he would later report. "One officer who was shot from his horse lay in a hollow place in the ground rolling and writhing in his blood."

One thousand American troops rushed to join Mercer's men, but well-aimed, intense British cannon and musket fire soon had the Americans retreating. Washington was watching the action with growing anxiety. If the retreat turned into another rout, his raid on Princeton — and the American Revolution — would be in jeopardy. Without a moment's hesitation, Washington spurred his horse into a headlong gallop toward the very center of the battle.

An instant later, he rode into the middle of the retreating men and took charge. "Parade with us, my brave fellows!" he called out to them.

On Long Island and again on Manhattan Island, his soldiers had ignored his commands to stand and fight. But the recent victories had renewed their trust in Washington. Instead of fleeing, they turned and followed Washington as he slowly advanced toward the British cannons.

If any of his men were scared, they did not show it. They admired Washington's courage and the fact that he had been with them every step of the way since New York. One American officer wrote to his wife, "O, my Susan! I shall never forget what I felt at Princeton on his account, when I saw him brave all the dangers of the field and his important life hanging as it were by a single hair with a thousand deaths flying around him."

Other American soldiers saw Washington bravely moving toward the enemy and rushed to be with him. As Washington approached within thirty paces of the enemy, the British lines raised their weapons, prepared to unleash a killing volley. Washington, sitting tall on his large horse, was a very easy target for the enemy.

A thousand tongues of fire leaped from the British musket barrels, accompanied by a thunderous roar and a wall of choking white smoke. At the same instant, the American soldiers fired as well. For twenty or thirty seconds the entire scene of the battle was hidden from view. One of Washington's young aides covered his eyes, expecting to find his commander shot from his horse.

The cloud of smoke slowly thinned to reveal the battlefield. Several of Washington's officers gasped. Many soldiers on both sides had been wounded or killed. But luck was once again with the old fox. Washington was still sitting astride his horse, still urging his men forward.

Moments later, the British soldiers saw that they were outnumbered by the oncoming Americans. They turned and ran for safety, and Washington and his army had secured another amazing victory.

These battles did not end the Revolution, but they did change the war dramatically. The idea that the British army was invincible was gone. George Washington and his ragtag amateur army had bested the enemy convincingly three times.

Even the British and their allies were impressed.

A Hessian captain confessed that when they finally reached Princeton after the American victory, "everyone was so frightened that it was completely forgotten even to obtain information about where the Americans had gone."

Maybe even more important, the spirit of revolution had been revived and given new energy. One disgruntled British Loyalist noted, "A few days ago they had given up the cause for lost. Their late successes have turned the scale, and now they are all liberty mad again."

There was a dramatic surge in enlistments following these American victories. In New Jersey, the militia had barely mustered 1,000 men during Washington's sad retreat through the state in December. By early spring of 1777, more than 17,000 had volunteered to fight.

What is more, these militia units became much more aggressive in attacking the remaining British outposts. Supported by members of the Continental army, the Americans intercepted and attacked every British patrol and supply party they came across. One by one, General Howe disbanded the garrisons and withdrew the men until, by spring, he had only two garrisons in New Jersey.

The hard, prolonged fighting, plus disease, caused a sharp drop in British troop strength as well. In August 1776, Howe had 34,000 men in his army; by the end of January 1777, he could count only 14,000 soldiers healthy enough to go into battle.

The war would go on for four more long years, with George Washington maintaining a hit-and-run style of fighting and avoiding head-to-head battles as often as possible.

This painting shows the moment when Washington entered the fight at Princeton to rally his troops. The British are to the right behind the wood fence. (THE HISTORICAL SOCIETY OF PENNSYLVANIA COLLECTION, ATWATER KENT MUSEUM OF PHILADELPHIA)

Then, late in 1781, Washington, with help from French forces, was able to trap 8,000 British soldiers at Yorktown, Virginia. The British commander, General Charles Cornwallis, surrendered on October 20. Two years later, the British signed a peace agreement, officially recognizing the United States as a free and independent country.

It had been a long, desperate journey for America's people, its soldiers, and especially for the commander of the army. During that time, Washington had transformed himself and his men. As one historian has said, when George Washington first took command of the American forces, he had been a "baffled, indecisive, disorganized, undisciplined leader." By 1781, he had delivered America from the "black times of Seventy-six" and created an organized, disciplined army willing to follow him into the most dangerous situations. Out of this, a new nation was born, and with it, the man who would lead it into the future.

A portrait of Washington done by James Peale after one painted by his brother, Charles Willson Peale. The dark left side represents the "black times" of the retreat through New Jersey; the brighter right side shows the ultimate American victory at Yorktown.

(INDEPENDENCE NATIONAL HISTORICAL PARK)

Washington Crossing the Delaware by Emanuel Leutze (1851)

(THE GRANGER COLLECTION, NEW YORK)

THE PAINTING

IN 1850, a thirty-four-year-old German artist named Emanuel Gottlieb Leutze finished a giant painting that was twelve feet high and twenty feet wide. Leutze named it *Washington Crossing the Delaware*. (See pp. 82–83.)

Leutze hoped his work would inspire fellow Europeans to fight against their oppressive governments just as the Americans had. Originally, Leutze had used bright colors in his painting to symbolize hope and triumph. However, before his painting was completed, the European revolutions in France, Germany, Hungary, and other countries failed. The artist then darkened the colors so that it focused less on the victory over oppression and more on the hard struggle for freedom.

Not long after Leutze finished *Washington Crossing the Delaware*, a fire broke out in his study and damaged the painting. The smoke and fire created a ghostly white haze that hovered around the figure of George Washington, while the other men remained sharp. Despite the damage, Leutze's work won a gold medal in a Berlin art show and drew large crowds throughout Europe. It then became a permanent part of the Bremen Art Museum collection, where it stayed until September 1942, when it was destroyed in a British bombing raid.

Fortunately, Leutze made a full-sized copy of *Washington Crossing the Delaware* in 1851 and sent it to America, where it traveled from city to city. In New York alone, more than 50,000 people came to view the painting. Eventually, it was bought by a private art collector in 1897, who then donated it to the Metropolitan Museum of Art.

Art historians have long criticized the painting as being factually inaccurate. They point out that the flag is wrong (the Stars and Stripes wasn't adopted until 1777), that the boat isn't the type actually used, that the crossing took place at night, and that if Washington had really stood during the journey he would probably have been tossed into the frigid waters. Such criticism might be correct, but it misses the point that Leutze was trying to make.

Leutze has packed the small boat with thirteen people, each dressed a little differently. Their clothes tell us that they descend from people from all over the world and come from many parts of America. There is a Scottish immigrant wearing a Balmoral bonnet, farmers from New Jersey and Pennsylvania in broad-brimmed hats, western riflemen in hunting shirts and deerskin leggings. One figure has a loose-fitting, flowing red shirt and might be a woman in disguise. There is even a man wearing the short tarpaulin jacket of a New England seaman, who happens to be of African descent.

Dominating the painting are two gentlemen officers. The one holding the flag up against the raging storm is a future president of the United States, James Monroe. The other, of course, is George Washington, who stands unblinking, looking through the snow and haze at the distant shore, as if peering into America's future.

These individuals are quite literally crammed into the same fragile boat, struggling to push their way past every obstacle to reach their goal of freedom. To accomplish this they have to work together in a disciplined, organized way, all the while being guided by their steady and unwavering leader, George Washington.

On the day that the actual crossing took place, Washington wrote a message on a tiny scrap of paper. The simple words were:

Victory or Death

In Leutze's painting, all of the power and purpose of those words can be found on the faces of the patriots as they struggle against seemingly insurmountable odds.

T I M E L I N E

This is a brief timeline of our Revolutionary War.

More complete timelines, along with related links, can be found at these websites:

http://www.historyplace.com/unitedstates/revolution/rev-prel.htm
http://www.nps.gov/archive/cowp/timeline.htm
http://www.ushistory.org/declaration/revwartimeline.htm
http://www.socialstudiesforkids.com/articles/ushistory/revolutionarywartimeline.htm

1754–1763:

The French and Indian War is fought. The war, plus an economic depression, creates a huge debt for Great Britain and prompts it to look to the colonies as a source of money.

1763–1767:

The British Parliament passes a number of laws that many colonists feel tax them unfairly or infringe on their personal freedoms. These include the Sugar Act and the Currency Act [1764], the Stamp Act and the Quartering Act [1765], the Declaratory Act [1766], and the Townshend Revenue Acts [1767].

1765:

[OCTOBER 7] The Stamp Act Congress is convened to formally protest this law.

1768:

[AUGUST 1] Boston merchants initiate the Non-Importation Agreement to stop buying British goods.

1770:

[MARCH 5] The Boston Massacre takes place.

1773:

[MAY 10] The British Parliament passes the Tea Act, taxing all imported tea to the colonies and requiring all tea to be sold by officially appointed British agents.

[DECEMBER 16] The Boston Tea Party takes place to protest the Tea Act.

1774:

[BETWEEN MARCH AND JUNE] The "Intolerable Acts" are imposed, closing down Boston Harbor and restricting the legal rights of American colonists. Also, all colonists are required to feed and house British troops under a new version of the Quartering Act.

[SEPTEMBER 5 TO OCTOBER 26] The First Continental Congress meets in Philadelphia and issues the Declaration and Resolves asserting the rights of the colonists, including the rights to "life, liberty, and property."

1775:

[APRIL 19] The Battles of Lexington and Concord take place. Following these battles, the British forces in Boston come under siege by American farmer-soldiers.

[MAY 10] Benedict Arnold, Ethan Allen, and the Green Mountain Boys seize Fort Ticonderoga and have the captured artillery transported to Boston.

[MAY 10] The Second Continental Congress meets in Philadelphia.

[JUNE 15] It appoints George Washington commander in chief of the Continental army.

[JUNE 17] The British defeat American forces in the Battle of Bunker Hill but suffer 1,054 casualties in the fight.

1776:

[MARCH 17] The British evacuate Boston.

[JULY 4] The Continental Congress adopts the Declaration of Independence.

[AUGUST 27] The British defeat George Washington's army in the Battle of Long Island.

[SEPTEMBER 15] The British occupy New York City.

[SEPTEMBER 16] The Continental army holds off initial British attacks at the Battle of Harlem Heights, but eventually it is forced to retreat to White Plains.

[OCTOBER 28] The Americans retreat from White Plains.

[NOVEMBER 16] Fort Washington is captured.

[NOVEMBER 20] Fort Lee is captured by British General Charles Cornwallis.

[DECEMBER 7] General Washington retreats with his army through New Jersey and crosses the Delaware into Pennsylvania.

[DECEMBER 13] While away from his troops, General Charles Lee is captured by the British at Basking Ridge, New Jersey.

[DECEMBER 26] Washington and what is left of his army re-cross the Delaware and capture Trenton.

1777:

[JANUARY 2] The Second Battle of Trenton is fought. The Continental army holds off a far larger British force, but eventually withdraws from its position.

[JANUARY 3] Washington defeats the British forces at Princeton and then goes into winter quarters in Morristown, New Jersey.

[SEPTEMBER 11] The British win the Battle of Brandywine in Pennsylvania against Washington's army.

[SEPTEMBER 19] General Horatio Gates and his army fight British General John Burgoyne to a draw in the first Battle of Saratoga.

[OCTOBER 4] Washington's troops are driven off at the Battle of Germantown.

[OCTOBER 7] Burgoyne loses the second Battle of Saratoga, mostly because of the heroic battlefield actions of Benedict Arnold.

[OCTOBER 17] Burgoyne surrenders and 5,700 British and Hessian soldiers are taken prisoners.

[DECEMBER 19] Washington takes his army into winter quarters at Valley Forge.

1778:

[FEBRUARY 6] The United States and France sign the French Alliance and France enters the war against Great Britain.

[JUNE 18] British forces abandon Philadelphia and retreat to New York City.

[JUNE 28] Washington's troops fight the British to a draw at the Battle of Monmouth Court House.

1779:

[JUNE 21] Spain declares war on Great Britain.

[NOVEMBER] Washington's troops winter at Morristown during one of the harshest winters on record.

1780:

[SEPTEMBER 25] Benedict Arnold's plan to surrender West Point to the British is discovered and he flees to British-held New York.

1781:

[JANUARY 1] Pennsylvania soldiers mutiny over lack of pay.

[SEPTEMBER 15] The French fleet defeats the British navy and drives it from Chesapeake Bay.

[OCTOBER 19] British General Charles Cornwallis is surrounded by American and French forces at Yorktown and surrenders to Washington.

1782:

[NOVEMBER 30] The Americans and British sign the preliminary Articles of Peace.

1783:

[APRIL 19] Congress ratifies the preliminary Articles of Peace.

[SEPTEMBER 3] The United States and Great Britain sign the Treaty of Paris.

[NOVEMBER 25] British troops leave New York City.

[DECEMBER 23] Washington resigns as commander in chief of the American forces.

1787:

[SEPTEMBER 17] The U.S. Constitution is signed.

1788:

[JUNE 21] The U.S. Constitution is ratified.

REVOLUTIONARY WAR SITES

IN NEW JERSEY, NEW YORK, AND PENNSYLVANIA

What follows is a handful of Internet sources that feature important Revolutionary War sites (battlefields, buildings, and terrain) mentioned in this book. Most contain directions and other information for visiting them. They also have photographs or virtual tours as well as interesting historical information.

NEW YORK

A very nice overview of numerous Revolutionary War sites in New York City can be found at NY Freedom Trail: http://www.nyfreedom.com/

Nothing is left of the original Fort Washington, but the landscape is dramatic and features a red lighthouse: http://www.nycgovparks.org/parks/fortwashingtonpark

Washington was very nearly captured at the Robert Morris House, now known as the Morris-Jumel Mansion: http://www.morrisjumel.org/

The capture of Fort Ticonderoga was one of the first victories for Revolutionary War forces: http://www.fort-ticonderoga.org/

The two Battles of Saratoga were the turning point of the Revolutionary War and very nearly made General Horatio Gates commander of all American forces: http://www.nps.gov/sara/index.htm

NEW JERSEY

While in Morristown for the winters of 1777 and 1780, George Washington had his headquarters at the Ford House, several miles away from where his troops stayed: http://www.nps.gov/morr/index.htm

Accommodations for Washington's troops were not quite so cozy and are located in what is now known as Morristown National Historical Park: http://www.nps.gov/morr/index.htm

Monmouth Battlefield State Park contains one of the best-preserved Revolutionary War battlefields: www.state.nj.us/dep/parksandforests/parks/monbat.html

Princeton Battlefield State Park can be found at: www.state.nj.us/dep/parksandforests/parks/princeton.html

Fort Lee Historic Park: www.njpalisades.org/flhp.htm

The Old Barracks were built in 1753 by the Colony of New Jersey for use by British soldiers during the French and Indian War. During the Revolutionary War it was used by British and Hessian troops and later by American soldiers. The Old Barracks Museum can be found at: http://www.barracks.org/

During the Battle of Princeton some savage fighting took place near Princeton University's Nassau Hall: http://princeton.edu/main/news/archive/S13/52/88S74

Washington's landing in New Jersey can be visited at Washington's Crossing State Park: http://www.state.nj.us/dep/parksandforests/washcros.html

PENNSYLVANIA

Washington was thoroughly outgeneraled at Brandywine but escaped to preserve his army: http://www.thebrandywine.com/attractions/battle.html

The winters in Morristown, NJ, were particularly brutal, but the Continental army's stay at Valley Forge is probably more famous: http://www.revolutionaryday.com/usroute202/philadelphia

You can see where Washington and his forces left Pennsylvania for the attack on Trenton at Washington Crossing Historic Park: http://www.ushistory.org/washingtoncrossing

Philadelphia has many notable Revolutionary War sites, including Independence National Historical Park, which features Independence Hall and the Liberty Bell: http://www.nps.gov/inde/index.htm

A nice look at a variety of other Philadelphia Revolutionary War locations can be found on this travel guide to Revolutionary War sites in a variety of states. Click on Route 202 and check out Old Philadelphia: http://www.revolutionaryday.com/usroute202/philadelphia

NOTES AND SOURCES

(IN ORDER OF IMPORTANCE)

It took a number of years to gather information for this book. Among the most helpful sources about the origins of the American Revolution and the events leading up to the battle of Trenton were:

Washington's Crossing by David Hackett Fischer. New York: Oxford University Press, 2006.

A Short History of the American Revolution by James L. Stokesbury. New York: William Morrow and Company, Inc., 1991.

Origin of the American Revolution, 1759–1766 by Bernhard Knollenberg. New York: Macmillan, 1960.

Thousands of books have been written about George Washington and his leadership of the Continental army. Here is a partial list of the works consulted:

George Washington: A Biography by Douglas Southall Freeman. New York: Charles Scribner's Sons, 1948–1957.

His Excellency: George Washington by Joseph J. Ellis. New York: Alfred A. Knopf, 2004.

George Washington in the American Revolution, 1775–1783 by James T. Flexner. Boston: Little, Brown and Company, 1968.

An Imperfect God: George Washington, His Slaves, and the Creation of America by Henry Wiencek. New York: Farrar, Straus and Giroux, 2003.

The Road to Valley Forge: How Washington Built the Army that Won the Revolution by John Buchanan. Hoboken, NJ: John Wiley & Sons, 2004.

Washington's Indispensable Men: The 32 Aides-de-Camp Who Helped Win American Independence by Arthur S. Lefkowitz. Mechanicsburg, PA: Stackpole Books, 2002.

A Revolutionary People at War: The Continental Army and American Character by Charles Royster. Chapel Hill, NC: W. W. Norton & Company, 1979.

The Continental Army by Robert K. Wright. Washington, DC: Center of Military History, United States Army, 1989.

After the disastrous campaigns in the autumn of 1776, Washington put a great deal of energy and money into gathering information about the opposing army. For more information about Washington's network of spies, these two books are very good sources:

Turncoats, Traitors & Heroes: Espionage in the American Revolution by John Bakeless. New York: Da Capo Press, 1998.

General Washington's Spies on Long Island and in New York by Morton Pennypacker. Brooklyn, NY: Long Island Historical Society, 1939.

To learn more about the details of opening battles of the Revolution, the following list of books is very useful:

The Battle for New York: The City at the Heart of the American Revolution by Barnet Schecter. New York: Penguin Books, 2003.

The Campaign of 1776 Around New York and Brooklyn by Henry Phelps Johnston. Brooklyn, NY: Long Island Historical Society, 1878.

General John Glover and His Marblehead Mariners by George A. Billias. New York: Holt, Rinehart and Winston, 1960.

The Revolutionary War in the Hackensack Valley: The Jersey Dutch and the Neutral Ground by Adrian C. Leiby. New Brunswick, NJ: Rutgers University Press, 1962.

The Long Retreat: The Calamitous American Defense of New Jersey, 1776 by Arthur S. Lefkowitz. New Brunswick, NJ: Rutgers University Press, 1999.

The Day Is Ours! November 1776–January 1777: An Inside View of the Battles of Trenton and Princeton by William M. Dwyer. New York: Penguin Books, 1983.

The Battles of Trenton and Princeton by William S. Stryker. Spartanburg, SC: Reprint Company, 1967.

The Christmas Campaign: The Ten Days of Trenton and Princeton by Kemble Widmer. Trenton, NJ: New Jersey Historical Commission, 1975.

A Brief Narrative of the Ravages of the British and Hessians at Princeton, 1776–77: A Contemporary Account of the Battles of Trenton and Princeton edited by Varnum Lansing Collins. Princeton, NJ: Princeton University Library, 1906.

The Trenton Commanders: Johann Gottlieb Rall and George Washington edited by Bruce E. Burgoyne. Bowie, MD: Heritage Books, 1997.

I've tried to allow the officers and soldiers involved in the battles covered in this book to speak for themselves as much as possible. Quotes were drawn from a great number of titles, including:

The Spirit of 'Seventy-Six: The Story of the American Revolution as Told by the Participants by Henry Steele Commager and Richard B. Morris. New York: Da Capo Press, 1995.

Rebels and Redcoats: The American Revolution Through the Eyes of Those Who Fought and Lived It by George F. Scheer and Hugh F. Rankin. New York: Da Capo Press, 1957.

The Revolution Remembered: Eyewitness Accounts of the War for Independence edited by John C. Dann. Chicago: University of Chicago Press, 1977.

Diary of a Common Soldier in the American Revolution, 1775–1783 edited by Robert C. Bray and Paul E. Bushnell. DeKalb, IL: Northern Illinois University Press, 1978.

A Narrative of a Revolutionary Soldier: Some of the Adventures, Dangers, and Sufferings by Joseph Plumb Martin. Hallowell, MD: privately printed, 1830.

A Narrative of Events, as They Occurred from Time to Time, in the Revolutionary War, with an Account of the Battles of Trenton, Trenton-Bridge, and Princeton by Joseph White, originally published in Charlestown, MA, in 1833, reprinted in *American Heritage*, June 1956.

Two books provided the information about Emanuel Leutze and his historic portrait of the crossing:

Portrait of Patriotism: Washington Crossing the Delaware by Ann Hawkes Hutton. Radnor, PA: Chilton Company, 1959.

Emanuel Leutze, 1816–1868 by Barbara S. Groseclose. Washington, DC: Smithsonian Books, 1975.

INDEX

PAGE NUMBERS IN BOLD INDICATE ILLUSTRATIONS